TELL ME MORE! science
MAGNIFICENT MOTHS

by Ruth Owen

Ruby Tuesday Books

Published in 2021 by Ruby Tuesday Books Ltd.

Copyright © 2021 Ruby Tuesday books Ltd.

All rights reserved. No part of this publication may be reproduced in whole or in part, stored in any retrieval system, or transmitted in any form or by any means, electronic, mechanical, photocopying, recording, or otherwise, without written permission from the publisher.

Consultant: Ross Piper
Designer: Emma Randall
Editor: Mark J. Sachner
Production: John Lingham

Photo credits:
Alamy: 7 (top), 22 (bottom); Public Domain: 12 (bottom); Istockphoto: Cover; Nature Picture Library: 15, 19, 20; Shutterstock: 1, 4–5, 6, 9, 10–11, 13, 14, 15 (top), 16–17, 18, 21, 22 (top), 23; Superstock: 8, 12 (top).

Library of Congress Control Number: 2020946818
Print (hardback) ISBN 978-1-78856-153-2
Print (paperback) ISBN 978-1-78856-154-9
eBook ISBN 978-1-78856-155-6

Printed and published in the United States of America
For further information including rights and permissions requests, please contact: **shan@rubytuesdaybooks.com**

Contents

What Is a Moth? 4

Moth or Butterfly? 6

A Moth's Life Cycle 8

How Many Legs? 10

Becoming an Adult 12

A Caterpillar Web 14

Feeding from Flowers 16

Living on a Sloth! 18

Hiding from Predators 20

Be a Moth Scientist 22

Glossary 23

Index, Read More, Answers 24

What Is a Moth?

Moths are insects that live in backyards, forests, deserts, and even on mountaintops.

A moth has two pairs of wings, six legs, and a pair of **antennae**.

Like all insects, a moth has a body in three main parts called the head, thorax, and abdomen.

Antennae

Head

Thorax

Abdomen

4

Fore (front) wing

Hind (back) wing

A moth's wings are made from thousands of tiny, colorful **scales** that overlap like the shingles on a roof.

Moth wing scales

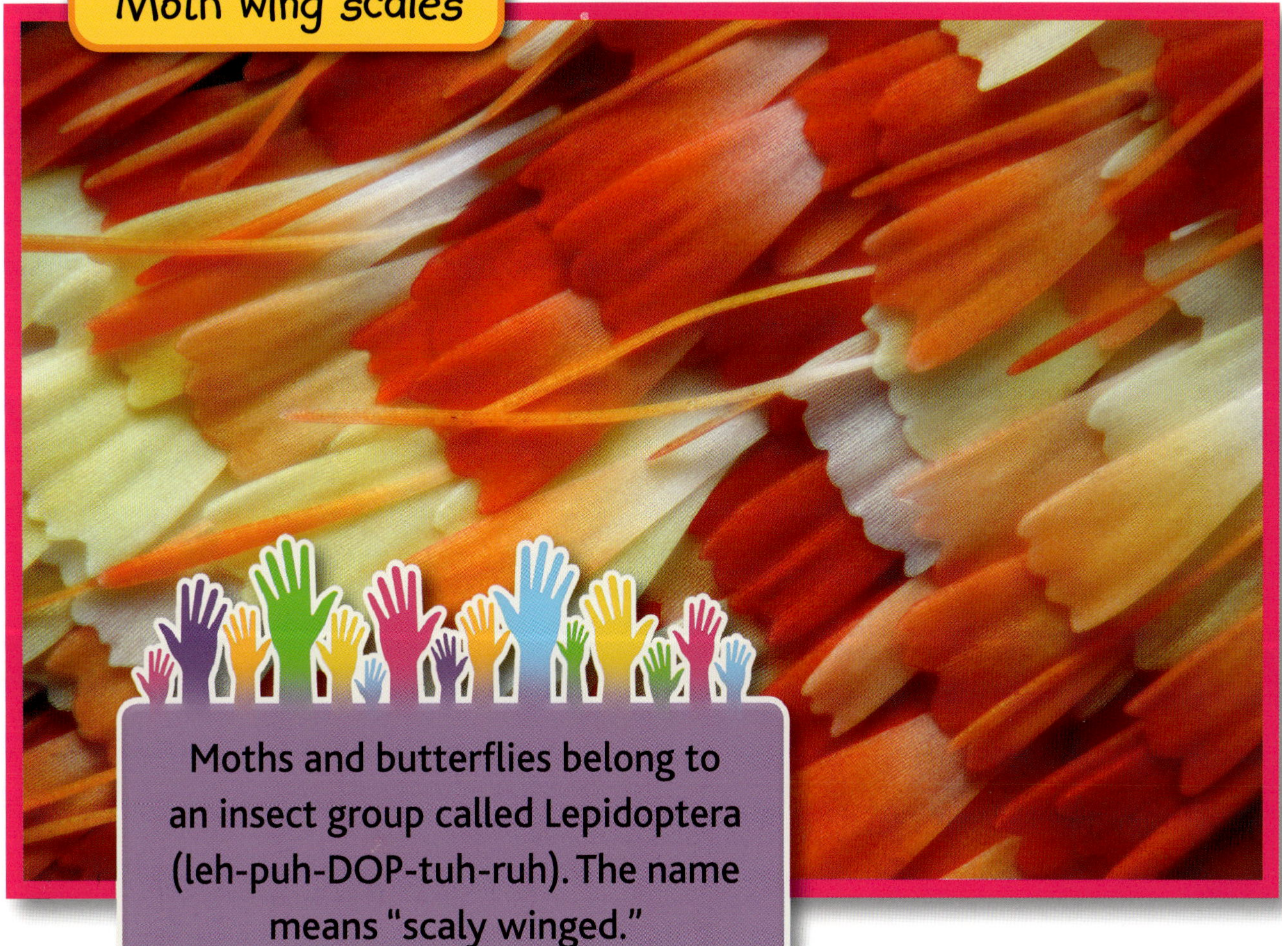

Moths and butterflies belong to an insect group called Lepidoptera (leh-puh-DOP-tuh-ruh). The name means "scaly winged."

Moth or Butterfly?

What is the difference between a moth and a butterfly? There are lots of ideas out there. Let's investigate them!

Moths are not as colorful as butterflies. Not true! Many moths are brightly colored.

All moths have feathery antennae. Wrong! Some moths have long, thin antennae, like butterflies.

Madagascan sunset moth

Moths only fly at night. False! Some moths are active in the daytime.

Scarlet tiger moth

Smooth body

Moths have furry bodies and butterflies have smooth bodies. Wrong! Some moths have smoother bodies and some butterflies are furry.

Moths have a tiny hook that joins their front and back wings. Butterflies don't have this. Scientists look for this hook to help them tell moths and butterflies apart.

The truth is that it's actually quite tricky to tell what is a moth and what is a butterfly.

7

A Moth's Life Cycle

Moths have a life cycle in four stages—egg, caterpillar, **pupa**, and adult.

After mating, most female moths lay their eggs on a plant.

Egg

This cecropia (suh-CROW-pee-uh) moth caterpillar is hatching.

A tiny caterpillar hatches from each egg.

Most caterpillars start eating plants and soon grow too big for their skins, or **exoskeletons**.

When this happens, a caterpillar's skin splits open, and underneath is a new, bigger skin.

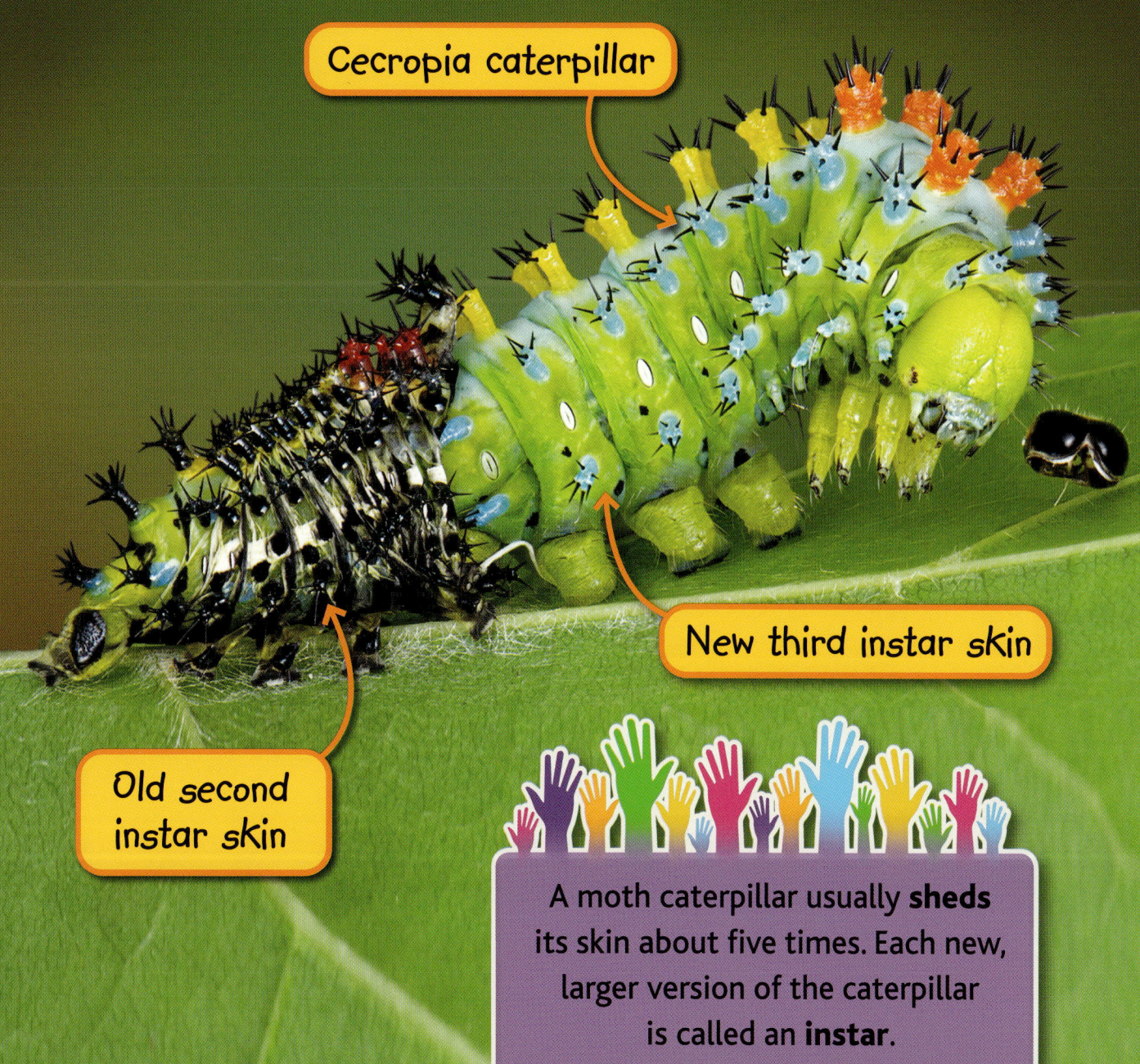

Cecropia caterpillar

New third instar skin

Old second instar skin

A moth caterpillar usually **sheds** its skin about five times. Each new, larger version of the caterpillar is called an **instar**.

How Many Legs?

Just like an adult moth, a caterpillar has three pairs of legs.

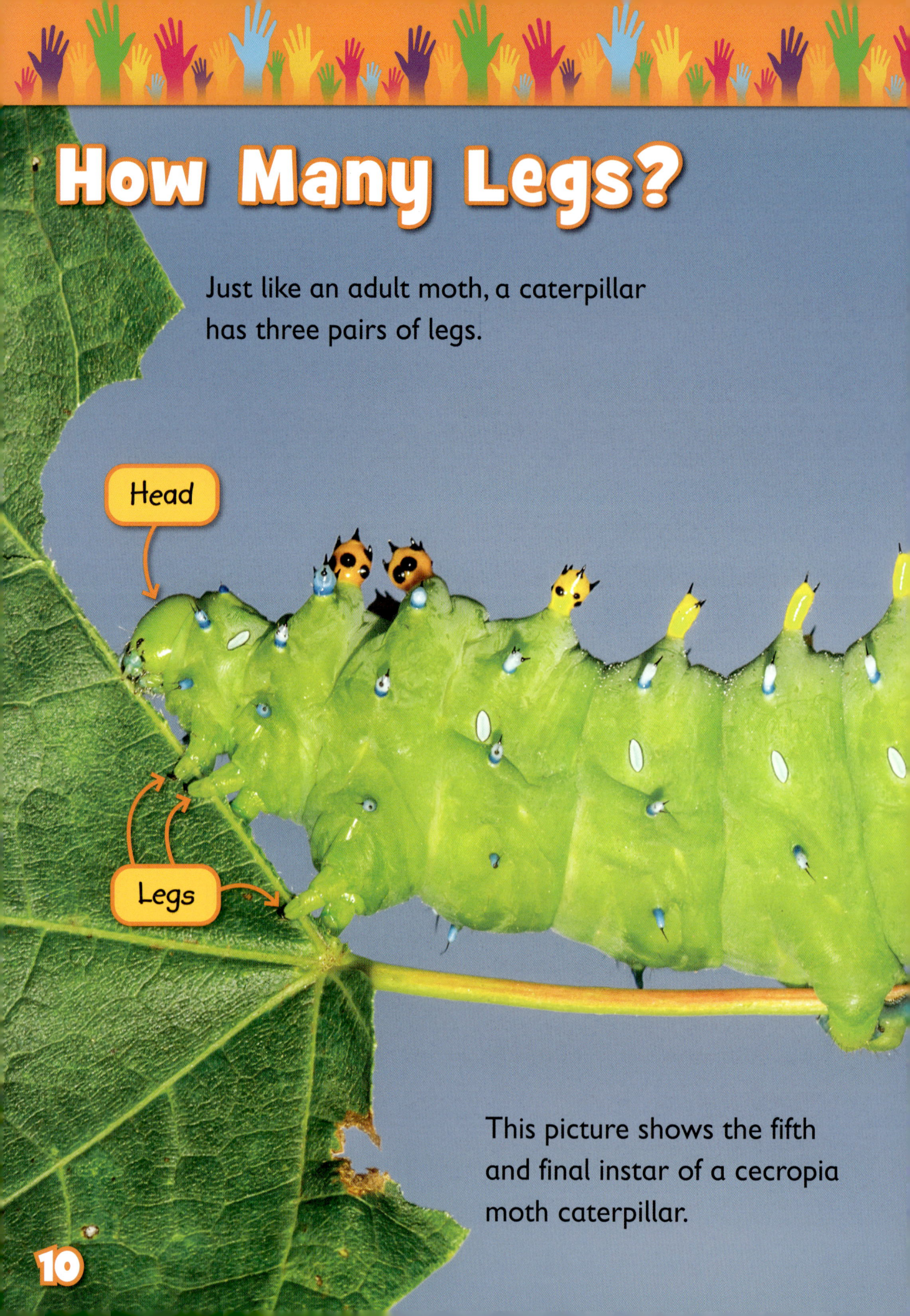

Head

Legs

This picture shows the fifth and final instar of a cecropia moth caterpillar.

10

A caterpillar also has stubby body parts called prolegs that help it move.

Adult moths do not have prolegs.

Prolegs

On the bottom of each proleg there are tiny hooks that grip onto plants—just like Velcro.

Becoming an Adult

When a caterpillar is ready to become an adult moth, it spins a silk **cocoon**.

It makes the silk inside its body and releases it from its mouth.

Caterpillar

Silk cocoon

Inside the cocoon, the caterpillar sheds its skin and becomes a pupa.

Pupa

Finally, the adult moth breaks out of the pupa skin and the cocoon.

Antennae

Adult cecropia moth

Moths use their antennae to **detect** the smell of food. Male moths can also detect special smells made by females who are ready to **mate**—even if they are 5 miles (8 km) away!

A Caterpillar Web

A bird cherry ermine moth lays her eggs on a bird cherry tree.

The leaves of this tree are the favorite food of her caterpillars.

A bird cherry ermine moth

Lots of females may lay their eggs on the same tree.

When the caterpillars hatch, they spin a giant silk web.

Feeding from Flowers

Most adult moths feed on **nectar** from flowers.

They drink through a straw-like mouthpart called a **proboscis** (pro-BOS-iss).

Antenna

Eye

Curled-up proboscis

Some types of moth only eat when they are caterpillars. Once they are adults, they do not eat, and only live for up to two weeks.

A hummingbird hawkmoth hovers over flowers drinking nectar—just like a tiny hummingbird.

It beats its wings so fast, they make a humming noise and look like a blur.

Proboscis

Hummingbird hawkmoth

Let's Talk
How do you think moths help flowers?
(The answer is on page 24.)

Living on a Sloth!

The sloth moth lives high in rain forest trees in the fur of three-toed sloths.

About once a week, a sloth climbs down to the ground to poop.

A three-toed sloth

The female moths fly from their sloth **host** and lay their eggs in the poop.

When the caterpillars hatch, they live in the poop and feed on it!

A baby sloth

Once a sloth moth caterpillar becomes an adult moth, it flies up into the treetops to find its own sloth host to live on.

Sloth moths in a mother sloth's fur.

Hiding from Predators

Moths and their caterpillars are food for birds, bats, and other animals.

But some moths have ways to fool their hungry **predators**.

A bagworm moth caterpillar builds a protective house of silk and twigs. As the caterpillar moves around feeding, all its predators see is a pile of twigs!

The caterpillar is under here.

Buff-tip moth's head

Wings with bark pattern

Real broken twig

When a buff-tip moth closes its wings, it looks just like a piece of broken twig.

An io (EYE-oh) moth

Some moths have a pattern on their wings that looks like two big eyes.

Let's Talk
How do you think the eye pattern protects the moth?
(The answer is on page 24.)

Be a Moth Scientist

You may have noticed that moths are attracted to bright lights. Why is this?

Moths may use the Moon to direct their flight. When a moth detects a bright porch light or street light, it may act as if the light is the Moon. The moth may get confused and flutter around as it tries to figure out where to fly. Eventually, it flies close to the light. Many scientists agree with this idea, but they can't say for sure if it is right.

For now, the question of why moths fly to bright lights still needs an answer!

Make a Moth Trap

Gather Your Equipment:
- A white sheet or piece of thin, white fabric
- Clothespins
- A flashlight

1. At night, pin the sheet to a clothesline.

2. Switch off any other outdoor lights and shine the flashlight onto the sheet.

3. Wait for moths to land on the sheet. Observe the moths, but do not touch them.

   How many different types of moths do you observe?

4. Take close-up photos of the moths. There are lots of good moth websites that will help you identify the moths you trapped.

Glossary

antennae
Two long body parts on the head of an insect that it uses for finding food, a mate, or for discovering other information about its world. The single word for these body parts is an antenna.

cocoon
A case in which some insects change from a larva into a pupa and then into an adult. A moth larva is known as a caterpillar.

detect
To discover or find something.

exoskeleton
The hard covering that protects the body of an insect.

host
An animal or plant on which other living things make their home.

instar
A stage in a caterpillar's life. Each instar is bigger than the one before and may also look different.

mate
To get together to produce young.

nectar
A sweet, sugary liquid produced by flowers. Nectar is food for insects, birds, bats, and other animals.

predator
An animal that hunts and eats other animals.

proboscis
A long, thin, tube-like mouthpart.

pupa
The stage in the life cycle of a moth when it changes from a caterpillar into a moth. Other types of insects also have a pupa stage.

scales
Small, flat sections of a material, such as skin, that overlap each other. The scales on a moth's wings are made of tough stuff called chitin.

shed
To get rid of something that's not wanted, such as an old skin.

An elephant hawk moth

Index

A
antennae 4, 6, 13, 16

B
bagworm moths 20
bird cherry ermine moths 14–15
buff-tip moths 21
butterflies 5, 6–7

C
caterpillars 8–9, 10–11, 12, 14–15, 16, 18–19, 20
cecropia moths 8–9, 10–11, 12–13
cocoons 12–13

E
eggs 8, 14, 18

F
food and feeding 8, 13, 14, 16–17, 18, 20

H
hummingbird hawkmoths 17

L
legs 4, 10–11

P
predators 20–21
pupa 8, 12–13

S
silk 12, 14–15, 20
sloth moths 18–19

W
wings 4–5, 7, 17, 21

Read More

Lawrence, Ellen. *A Butterfly's Life (Animal Diaries: Life Cycles)*. Minneapolis, MN: Bearport Publishing (2017).

Owen, Ruth. *Stag Beetle (Wildlife Watchers)*. Minneapolis, MN: Ruby Tuesday Books (2018).

Answers

Page 15:
The caterpillars build the web for protection. The web makes it difficult for hungry birds to reach the caterpillars to eat them.

Page 17:
Moths are pollinators that help flowers make seeds. When a moth lands on a flower to drink nectar, pollen sticks to its body. Then the moth flies to a different flower, and the pollen goes too. In order to make seeds, a flower needs pollen from another flower. Butterflies, bees, and many other insects are also pollinators.

Page 21:
Some moths have a pattern on their wings that looks like two eyes. When a predator goes to attack, it sees the big eyes and thinks the moth is a much larger animal. The predator may leave the moth alone and go elsewhere for its meal!